Love Is All-Forgiving

Love Is All-Forgiving

Reflections on Love and Spirituality

PETER DEUNOV

Compiled by Milka Kraleva

Translated into English by Janeta Shinkova
and edited by David Lorimer

Health Communications, Inc.
Deerfield Beach, Florida

www.bcibooks.com

Library of Congress Cataloging-in-Publication Data
is available from the Library of Congress

©2004 Kibea Publishing
ISBN 0-7573-0208-4

Publisher: Health Communications, Inc.
         3201 S.W. 15th Street
         Deerfield Beach, FL 33442-8190

R-10-04

Book cover designed by Larissa Hise Henoch
Inside book formatting Dawn Von Strolley Grove

Contents

Introduction

*T*he Bulgarian philosopher, Peter Deunov, (1864–1944), is re-nowned as one of the major spiritual leaders of the twentieth century.

His teachings were concerned with helping each of us overcome our internal conflicts and maintain better human relations through spiritual awareness and devotion to truth. Deunov regarded love as the most significant factor in human relations and throughout his life he sought to elucidate its essence. He spoke about love in all his talks and lectures describing it as a universal, life-sustaining force.

This book of maxims is selected from the rich heritage of Peter Deunov's philosophy.

The Essence of Love

*L*ove is the most important challenge of life. If you solve it, all other issues—private, social, family or universal— will be overcome.

*L*ove is a force that transforms everything and saves you. It comes, real and alive, to sweep away any obstacles. One who attains love enters the realm of reason.

Physical love is hugging and kissing. Real love is touching, while ideal love is only from a distance.

Physical love brings great changes. One who wants to experience it should know that it involves changes of the state of mind, from joy to grief and from grief to joy.

3

*D*ivine love performs miracles. Everywhere it goes, it creates and recreates. This love should be studied. But remember, if you have not learned human love, which involves lesser self-sacrifice, how can you learn divine love, which requires a great self-sacrifice?

*L*ove is something sublime. It is not a man's or a woman's feeling; what excites people and arouses their base nature is not love. What manifests now is distorted human life.

Love is the basis, the foundation of everything, for it is a virtue that is blind to human mistakes, and is never offended. Even in the worst mistakes it only sees something positive.

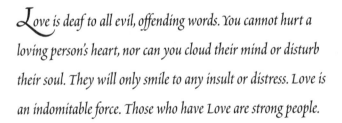

Love is deaf to all evil, offending words. You cannot hurt a loving person's heart, nor can you cloud their mind or disturb their soul. They will only smile to any insult or distress. Love is an indomitable force. Those who have Love are strong people.

You wish to show your love for someone but you are afraid of being fooled. Can love fear lies? The sun shines and brings warmth to all beings even though some of them do blameworthy things.

When light and love come from the same source there is no sin. Sin is where light and love come from different sources.

A love that is unable to survive any trial in life is not true love.

When in love, one faces a grim consecution of events that inevitably brings suffering. If you fall in love, you have to know that you will go through that sequence of deadly experiences. If your mind is alert, you will pass through it and learn something from it; if not, misfortunes that you have never imagined will befall you.

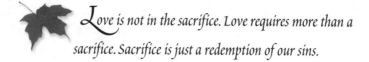

Love is not in the sacrifice. Love requires more than a sacrifice. Sacrifice is just a redemption of our sins.

There is no sin in love. Love is from God. Any love that elevates you comes from God.

The first characteristic of true love is your desire to place your beloved on your own level.

*L*ove precludes violence. It is present only when people act by their own free will. Everyone wants the freedom to decide to do something for their neighbor. Should you force them to do it, they will immediately resist.

*L*ove is the only force that acts without any bias. It opens your eyes instead of clouding them. When you love, you can see clearly. Only through love can you know people.

9

Love manifests in life outside time and space. It depends neither on time nor on external conditions. Love comes from a person's contact with God and is driven by an internal, inner impulse.

Love is the eternal aspiration of two souls.

People of love bring peace, joy and fun. Wherever they go, they are welcomed with open hearts. They are not ignorant, proud or ambitious but humble and sincere.

*O*nly the warmth of love can remove
all doubts, suspicions and disappointments
in life.

*T*he love that involves fear is not a true love. Love is the
only force in the world that knows no fear.

*L*ove has an immense power. It performs miracles. For love,
people are prepared to make sacrifices that they never would
make without love. Love elevates and improves one's life.
Therefore, whatever you do, do it with love.

11

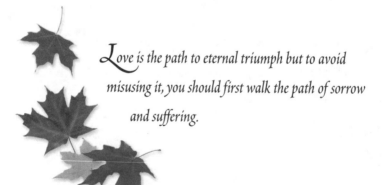

The transcendence of love lies in being loved by all creatures instead of just one.

What is blameworthy is ignorance, the misunderstanding and misuse of love. What is blameworthy is our striving to shackle love.

Love is the path to eternal triumph but to avoid misusing it, you should first walk the path of sorrow and suffering.

Love is the path of least resistance.
Divine souls never walk the path of love;
they walk the path of wisdom. If you wish to
avoid making mistakes, take the path of love. It is given
for the weak. Those with divine strength have no need for
love; it is the weak who need it.

The difference between human and divine love is that divine
love complements everything in human love without changing it.

13

*B*y love we should always mean the principle that gives
life. The only way that people can reach an agreement is
through love. When you enter its realm, you will become happy
and healthy, your life will acquire meaning, and you will be
ready to serve.

*W*here love is, where service is, there is paradise, there is
bliss, there is God, there is wealth.

*L*ove is never jealous, and it never asserts its rights.
It makes you attractive because it cares little about
pride.

*L*ove can be physical, mechanical, or
spiritual: these are three ways in which the
law of love transforms the forces in the world.

*L*ove is the cosmic force that invigorates the human
organism. Even in its lowest manifestation it harmonizes all
the body's organs and gives human life an impetus. Love is the
reason for the coming of light, warmth, science and good
relationships; it stimulates all of nature, the whole of humanity,
and it only can make the world a better place.

Love can be transmitted in physical, astral, mental, causal and innumerable other ways but the results are always the same. It brings light, warmth and freedom.

Love never forgets. Even if you leave this world, it will still be thinking of you.

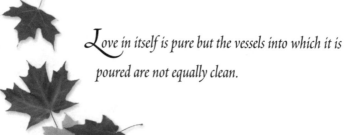

Love in itself is pure but the vessels into which it is poured are not equally clean.

16

Love does not care for consequences. It is ruled by a principle and as long as the principle is correct, the consequences will be right and good.

Love is not lasting because it is so strong that if it lasts you would be unable to endure its vibrations.

Love induces physical and mental transformation. It creates in you a series of alchemical processes under whose influence your entire self changes. Everyone changes when they feel that they are loved.

*T*hrough one's love of God one is born; through one's love of one's neighbor one grows.

*I*n love, there is an element that melts people: rich and poor, learned and ignorant alike. You may cry, you may grieve, you may be cheerful or desperate, but the point is that all fires and falls, all revivals and all flying are the result of love.

Love dislikes complaints; it does not care if you are ignorant, or poor, or a sinner; it throws you into the pot and melts you. No matter how you hide, no matter what you do to avoid it, it will find you. All that is left to you is to say: "Here I am for you!"

19

The Language
of Love

If you wish to love, you must not be afraid. If you wish to be loved, you must not have doubts.

If you love someone, do not talk about your love. The person whom you love should not know about your feelings.

People should not ask each other the question: "Do you love me?" What glows does not burn. Love does not speak.

If you are not prepared to sacrifice
everything in this world for love, you
cannot understand life. You must be ready for
sacrifices, not in terms of giving up life but rather for
seeing the positive and beautiful side of everything.

In whatever form love comes to you, be grateful. It has come
to clear away anything filthy that comes its way.

Love cannot be requested. One who demands love has no love
inside them.

$\mathcal{N}$o force can resist the person who has love. They have a new understanding and dwell in peace and light.

$\mathcal{T}$here is a special time for love. You can have feelings or be in a definite mood at any time, but to love in a way that allows you to change and be free of all instincts, to conquer the wolf, the tiger in yourself—this does not happen every time.

By wanting to possess something through your feelings, you create a karma. By setting people free, you free yourself from your karma.

You cannot love someone without having been related with them in the past. Love between people manifests in more than one life.

When two people love each other they add an impulse to something great in the entire cosmos.

You yourself create the way in which you will be loved. As you love, so will you be loved. As you do unto others, so will others do unto you.

When you love someone, set them free. To avoid creating a conflict in the person you love, give them freedom! Love will then manifest freely. If the person whom you love is free, you will be free as well.

*L*oving someone does not mean that they must be thinking of you. The person you love should have a character that is opposite to yours so that you may complement each other.

*O*ne who applies the law of love speaks little and does much.

*T*he meaning of life lies in finding the person who loves you and whom you love.

*W*hen you love someone, you listen to them without being bored, and you feel as if an elixir pours into you, invigorating and reviving you. When your beloved is gone, you think to yourself, "This person gave me so much." This is what loving and being loved means.

*E*ven if the person you love speaks ill of you and harms you, your feeling should not cease.

*W*ho should love: the strong or the
weak? The weak cannot love. Only the
strong can love.

*W*hen someone loves you, they foresee all your needs.

*W*hen you love someone you should think what good you
can do to them, how you can give them your love and satisfy
them. Only then will they know that you love them.

You cannot have faith without having love. Faith determines your love. Hope determines your faith. Love determines your mind.

If two people who love each other do not trust their minds and hearts, they will achieve nothing. Faith is the connecting thread in human life.

If you love and die, you will certainly come back to life. If you do not love, even though you breathe, you will be dead.

$\mathcal{L}$oving is a process of the heart in
which you develop your power. Being loved
is a process of the mind in which you develop
your knowledge.

One who loves, gives much. Loving requires giving and
receiving that involve no damage.

$\mathcal{T}$he person who loves you can heal you and teach you.
Loving is the greatest of arts.

31

It is an immense wealth to have someone's love! It means having someone with you on whom you may rely in any circumstances.

You should not avoid suffering; one benefits from reasonable suffering. However by accepting love you pass from suffering to joy in which you can develop properly.

Do not say you love someone more and another one less. Love with all the love your heart will yield.

*N*o one can force you to love. If
you do not have the inner impulse to
extend love to someone, no external reason can
make you do it.

*O*nly the one who loves you has something to give you. If
someone does not love you, they have nothing to give you.

*W*hen two people love each other they need to develop
simultaneously in body, heart and mind. There should be
harmony between them.

You should be open to everyone you love. You should be ready for any sacrifice. Love is the human soul's connection with God.

Every feeling that brings distress brings death. Every feeling that brings joy and fun brings life. The feeling that brings distress is not for you; the feeling that brings joy is for you: take it in!

If someone who does not love you caresses your head, you will feel unwell all day. But if you are caressed by someone who loves you and whom you love, you will be happy all day. A person who loves is a conduit for a divine energy that is beneficial to every living creature.

Life cannot improve without love, without good acts, without righteous and noble thoughts. Physical love should be a foreword to spiritual love. Spiritual love should be the preface to divine love.

The one who loves you is not here on earth. If he were, the two of you would be living in the same body. You do not know his name. Only when you are very sad and find yourself at crossroads, he will comfort you and go away again. This is for those who wish to be happy.

Everyone has someone destined to love them. Everyone must find the one who loves them.

When you love someone, you feel a sacred thrill about them. It is the sacred thrill of love. Everyone has experienced it. It is the only thing that can make you happy.

If the thought of a certain person is
forever on your mind, know that they love
you. If you are forever on their mind, you love
each other.

If in your mind you imagine that the person you love
might get you into trouble, it is a sign that you do not love
them.

Love can tolerate absolutely no lie. Those who attempt to
profane love go into decline.

37

*H*aving lost all his strength, health and wealth, the
person who endures without wincing, is a person who dwells
in love.

*I*n order truly to know people, you have to love them.

*I*f you love someone, you will become one with them, not
an object for them. If you become an object, you will
expose them to temptation.

*Y*ou cannot think of someone
unless they are also thinking of you.

*W*hen you love someone, you see your reflection in
them as in a mirror. When someone loves you, they see their
reflection in you as in a mirror.

*L*ove is manifested in giving and taking. One who loves
mostly gives, while one who is loved mostly takes.

*H*e who loves will be put in the hearth to burn. Those he loves will have warmth and light. Then they will go into the hearth for him to have warmth and light. People fail to understand this law and expect only to be loved. No such thing exists. You love and you are loved. There must be exchange in life.

*T*o be strong, you should be happy both externally and internally. If you are unhappy, your connection with love is severed.

*T*hink of your friend and if you feel
better, you do love them. If your condition
does not change, you do not love them. When
you love, you receive.

*T*here is no power in love. In it, there is something greater
than power. In love, you have energy for the person you love.
You can foresee everything they need.

*T*ake one's worst vice, throw it into the flames of love, and that instant it will turn into a gemstone.

*S*uffering precedes love. No one can experience love without passing through suffering first. When he does, he will find love, the greatest wealth in the world. It is worth passing through suffering to attain the greatest wealth. In that wealth lies human strength.

*S*orrow is the border to love. When
you come to the greatest sorrow, you will
have reached the border of the love that the
soul seeks.

*Y*ou have the right to love but not to possess. Nature does
not allow you to possess what it gives you. It will always resist
your attempt to conquer what it has created.

*W*hen you love someone, infidelity is nearly impossible. The one you love cannot betray you. When we talk of infidelity, we mean human love, the love of human beings on earth.

*I*f your love cannot overcome any hardship, what sort of a love is that?

*W*hen taking the right course, some feel nervous and uneasy. This is because love reforms their hearts and makes them more sensitive.

*I*n how many ways can you be
saved? There is but one way: the way of
love. If you believe in love and live by its laws,
you can be saved.

A smart person is one who knows when to retreat and
when to approach love.

*W*hen you work with love, you will first experience some
improvement that will give way to a decline, followed by a
greater improvement and a greater decline until you reach
the state of genuine health.

*R*emember that without going down there is no going up. One who refuses to go down does not want to go up. The two go together. When you reach divine love it will encourage you to give up heaven and come down to earth to help.

*W*hen you love someone, you are helping them, while at the same time promoting your own elevation.

*L*oving those who love you is human. Being benevolent to those who are not benevolent to you is divine.

*I*f the divine is at work in someone, you will inevitably love them. If they have allowed their human side to reign, you are bound to face great conflicts.

*L*ove makes you strong and powerful. While love is inside you, you need nothing outside you. No one outside you can preserve your love nor take it away. You will envelop your beloved with an aura of fire and mark: "Danger! Keep away!" Only thus can love protect life.

*T*he first sign of the arrival of love is suffering. The more the suffering, the closer love is.

It is not easy to keep others' love for you. If you think you can toy with someone's love and keep it, you are wrong.

You cannot love a person who has not a single virtue. For a learned person you may feel respect but not love. For a strong person you may feel awe but not love. A virtuous person, however, you can love.

49

*L*oving someone means having a continual feeling about them. A feeling is strong as long as it is uninterrupted. Even if the one you love abuses you and harms you, your feeling should go on uninterrupted.

*I*f you see the one you love suffer, you should be the first to come to their aid. This is love. If you do not help them, you do not love them. Love rectifies all mistakes.

*Y*our first love is the visit of an angel who takes you to the person you will fall in love with.

The ones who love you will come to
you. They will not wait for you to look for
them. If you see your loved ones abused, you
will be the first one to stand up for them!

Usually people long to be much loved—and to love
much. When does love show its strength? Under great
pressure!

When you love and are loved, there is a proper exchange
between the two of you. Then you both understand the action
of love. It is a force that operates in the spiritual world.

51

If you are angry, you will not achieve love. When you are angry, you are far from love. You cannot find love with suspicion and doubt.

If you love truly you are never sorry that you love even if you are not loved.

Love is an internal stimulus that urges you forward. Without love, you cannot make progress. Without anyone to love, you cannot learn. You need to love at least one living creature from whom you can learn.

There is no greater human experience than meeting a soul you can talk to, a soul from which you obtain something new and noble.

If you want someone to love you, follow this rule: find a good quality in that person, and keep it always in your mind.

There can be no relation between people until they are full of burning desire to help each other—help with thoughts and feelings as well as in a material sense.

*In the love between two people, energies need to cross.
The intensity of the one's heart should be equal to the
intensity of the other's mind, and vice versa.*

*The philosophy of love is giving and taking at the same time,
to achieve a proper exchange.*

*You cannot know love before you have passed through
the greatest conflicts and suffering in life.*

Love involves a proper energy
exchange between two beings who help
each other. If two people love each other but
cannot help each other, there is no exchange between
them.

Someone can love you as long as you give them freedom.
Should you take their freedom away, you break the law.
You have to deserve love.

Loving someone is to make them happy.

It does not matter if someone pays no attention to your love. One day they will appreciate what you have given them, and will respond to your love with love. They will pay more for what they have obtained from you. You may lose anywhere, in anything, but not in love.

If you suffer because someone does not love you, because their love for you has changed, you have to know that they never loved you.

If you do not love you cannot live. If people do not love you they cannot live.

Speaking of love, you must know whether you want to love or to be loved. If you want to love, start giving. Go to the person you love and help them with their work. When you love you give; when you are loved you will be given, and you will be receiving gratefully.

Only in the presence of the person who loves you, will your hardships wane and vanish.

57

*O*ne who loves must sacrifice a part of themselves. One who sacrifices intellectually is a true person, a person of love.

*I*f love weakens life, it is a weak love. If love makes life stronger, it is a strong love.

*L*oving someone who loves you is easy, but loving someone who doesn't requires strength. In the struggle, however, you will gain wisdom.

Loving is the noblest, most sublime
and most sacred action in life. If you do not
understand love you are ashamed of it and
you are sorry to have loved. In that way you break the
laws of love.

One who loves is always right.

Take from the person you love as much as you need at a
definite moment, but not more. If you take more than you need,
the exchange is disrupted and you cannot love each other.

Loving someone means giving them part of your feelings and your strength. This is the medium of exchange in the spiritual world. Always dwell where love dwells—there is no better place.

Everyone who loves and is loved is revived. No one can love you all by themselves. One who loves you has been urged by God, and if they follow that urge, they will be blessed.

*L*ove should be your master, and you
should be its disciple. You will then
understand that wherever love takes you, you
must not be afraid.

*Y*ou cannot grow without love.

*W*hen two people love each other they will depart together.
In the future, when two people love each other, they will not be
two persons but one.

61

*W*hen someone says they love, they should meet two
requirements: give without expecting anything in return
and love without expecting to be loved. When someone gives
and another takes, they should have a sacred feeling.
Love is that sacred feeling.

*A*ccording to the laws of love and nature, everyone should
be free to express themselves just as the spring flows freely.
The greatest evil comes from great restrictions. It is a
great thing not to impose restrictions.

*W*hen I talk of love I avoid
monotony. Love has many forms; it
involves a great variety. The love I am talking
about is now coming to the world. If you love someone
and they become a good person, only then do you love
them truly.

*L*oving those who love you is human. Loving those who do
not love you is divine.

*L*ove brings no anxiety. When you love someone and think
of them, you should have a pleasant feeling.

*I*n this world, there is nothing better than love. It is good to have someone to rely on completely and to trust completely, so that no fear may affect your soul in any vicissitudes of life.

*W*hen you love, you elevate yourself as well as the person you love.

*W*hen two people love each other and ignore everyone else, this is not love. You cannot love anyone without loving all people at the same time.

If you are discouraged, there is no love in you. You are strong when you love. When you fall in love you become a finer and nobler person, and you are ready to sacrifice yourself for your love.

One who loses everything to get to know life walks on the path of love. You should lose everything old to enter life anew.

You cannot be happy unless you love someone without them knowing that you love them. This is the only way you can be happy. There has to be someone onto whom you may pour out your feelings, just as a spring flows and waters the land around. When you love someone and you pour out your love for them, it will flow as life-giving water to the benefit of those around you. Do not reveal the name of the person for whom you are doing that.

Man and Woman

*T*he woman and the man are steps towards learning to
live with God. The woman is the negative, the man is the
positive principle. The genuine manifestation, however, is
always towards the negative; the current flows towards the
negative. Women are now the bearers of culture. The man is the
alpha, the woman is the omega of things; that is where all
energy is directed.

*T*wo women can live with the same man only if
one of them renounces in the other's favor.

The man is the condition for the woman's elevation, and the woman is the condition for the man's elevation. In the man, the woman looks for a sublime being from the divine world. The man must become a channel of the spirit because the woman seeks the spirit in the world. The woman's ideal is the spirit; the man's ideal is the soul.

You feel a genuine love and inspiration when you encounter a woman of spirit and soul, mind and heart. A man should be inspired by such a woman.

*I*f a woman can improve her husband's character, she has love. If a man can do the same for his wife, he has love.

A wife should never cry in front of her husband, nor a husband in front of his wife.

*W*hat does masculinity involve? I call a man the person who takes the side of the weak. I call a woman only the person who is able to dress the wounds of the suffering.

A man can reform a woman but
not by force. A woman can reform a man
but not with words. A woman reforms a man
with love, and a man reforms a woman with wisdom.

A woman needs freedom, given that she uses it as the
foundation for building her husband's happiness and health. If
a woman is not free, her husband is not happy.

If a man thinks he can impose his dogma on a woman, he is wrong. If a woman thinks she can impose her dogma on a man, she is wrong as well. Both men and women remain the way they have been born. A good woman was born good, and a good man was born good.

A man and a woman unite in order to develop. Marriage is necessary so that both the man and the woman may develop, acquire new qualities and study the laws.

The woman is the man's opposite. Only in the woman can the man see himself as he is. Only in the man can the woman see herself as she is. The man is the woman's mirror, and the woman is the man's mirror. With this understanding of the human being, men and women will not seduce each other and will not be unhappy with each other.

If the man speaks the truth, the woman will not distrust him.

If a man strikes a woman, the great astral snake-woman will come to teach him a lesson he will remember for years.

If men and women unite in the name of the laws that exist in nature, they can transform the world!

The Bulgarian word for "woman" is related to the Sanskrit word "zeo" which means "life". The word for "man" derives from the Sanskrit word "manas" which means a thinking being.

*T*he man is the cerebrum through which the human being is connected with the outside world. The woman is the solar plexus through which the human being is connected with the internal, divine world. The solar plexus is related to the entire universe, therefore the woman is closer to the divine world than the man. What you perceive with the solar plexus is truer than what you perceive with the cerebrum.

*W*ithout a man and a woman, there cannot be a human being. This is why everyone looks for a mate. You will look for your mate everywhere, and when you find each other, you will be married. This is what marriage is about, this is what a human being is about.

*T*he woman should come to the front of life to save the world. The man preaches, but the woman is the one who has to carry out what he preaches so that the world may be saved.

Today, people are afraid of
trivialities. The husband is afraid that his
wife might leave him, while the wife is afraid
that her husband might leave her. Why should they be
afraid? Who has brought them together? Only the link of
love is eternal and unbreakable. If the divine love connects
you, no force in the world can break that connection.

When a man loves a woman it is a gift of God for him and
a blessing for her.

*W*hen a man and a woman start living together, one of them will be a master and the other a disciple. Do not fight for supremacy. If the man has vibrations that may elevate the woman's mind, she should let him be the master instead of saying, "I hate to submit!" Submitting means receiving and processing energy. That is culture!

*I*t is of immense significance what sort of a person loves you. If you are loved by an ordinary person, you will become ordinary yourself. If you are loved by a talented person, you will become talented. If you are loved by a genius you will become a genius.

A man loves his wife as long as she
is healthy and beautiful. When she falls ill
and loses her beauty he will cease loving her.
The same applies to women. It is admirable to love a
sinful and ugly person. A strong person can love all people
and urge them towards what is good and beautiful in the
world.

*I*t is a strange thing when people talk about a man seeing a
woman. Even if he does, so what? God made them to see each
other. If God told them to love each other I am at their side.
The right attitude is not to meddle in other people's affairs.

*I*f a man has spare energy, let him direct it to another woman, but only in an intellectual way; if a woman has spare energy, let her direct it to another man, but similarly.

*T*he woman must not seek the man's love. She must be the source from which love flows. She must love instead of expecting to be loved!

If a man and a woman love each
other they are already married in the
divine world, no matter if they have any
written document here. In the invisible world, it is
important how you will stand love, whether you will
preserve it or will lose it in a couple of years.

If a woman regards life as a divine manifestation, she will
not feel restricted and will be able to solve problems correctly.
No man can restrict such a woman.

The woman must be stronger in the astral world while the man must be stronger in the mental world. When the woman enters the man's love, she should feel a pleasant wave of freshness from him, cooling her heat. Under her heat, everything grows and develops. The understanding and application of love, on the other hand, requires coolness to prevent the fruits from rotting.

Pieces of
Advice

Take down the icon of happiness and replace it with this motto: Love requires daring, courage and determination.

Do not run away from love but take it into you. Do not be afraid if your heart goes on fire. If an angel set fire to it, you will obtain something valuable.

In all circumstances, listen to your heart's voice and follow its path. The divine laws are written in the human heart.

*B*y loving someone I mean not
allowing into your mind a single thought
against them, and keeping their image as
sacred as your own. This is a maxim. Love this way if
you can.

*W*hen you love someone you cannot live without them.
This is love, its essential meaning. If you think you can live
without that someone, you do not love them.

If one day people cease loving each other, life will come to an end. Be grateful that people love each other. In every sense, love brings life.

If you want someone to love you, then set them free.

A brother is related by blood, while a friend is related by feelings. You should start from brotherhood and move towards friendship.

I often speak to you of the great
divine love but not all of you understand it.
Until you do, keep the old love. Seek to achieve
the new love but do not give up the old one. The old love
burns while the new love revives.

*D*o not let people experiment with your heart.

*A*pply love in life to overcome obstacles in both the physical
and the spiritual world.

*I*f your love for someone is too strong you will harm them. By thinking incessantly of them you disturb them because you control them with your thoughts. Loving someone means wishing them well and leaving them free.

*I*t is wrong to ask someone you love to pay for your love. You should be happy to have done them good.

$\mathcal{N}$ever be sorry to have loved and
never be sorry to have been loved.

$\mathcal{T}$o avoid losing your love, do not ask your partner how
long he will love you. Love is outside time and space. Think of
the moment when love smiles to you. If you think of the future,
you will suffer.

*N*ever suppress your feelings. Never force them. This
does not mean that you should do as you wish. Do not
suppress feelings but wait for them to mature.

*I*f you fall in love with someone, do not touch them. If you
fall in love with someone, tell them the truth that will bring
them light and will make them free.

If you wish to be happy in love, maintain a reasonable distance between yourself and your beloved. If you reduce this distance you will lose your love.

The divine laws are written in the heart. Therefore, do not attempt to rule anyone's heart, and do not allow anyone to rule yours.

*O*nce you have invited love to ride on your back, you
have to take it to the end of its journey. Heavy as it might be,
do not attempt to drop it because that will bring greater
misery. You will be carrying it, you will be stopping for a rest
and you will be carrying it again until it gets off your back. If
you made the mistake of letting love get onto your back, do not
make a second mistake by throwing it off. Endure to the end.

*I*f you love someone, be free and do not hide your
feelings. Water each flower as much as it needs.

*I*t is better to lose everything than corrupt love. As long as love is in you, you need nothing from the outside. Love makes you strong and powerful.

*D*o not doubt the person you love. Doubting is not love. He who loves has no doubts.

Believe only in love that gives.

I teach a great love, an active love, a love of kisses but also meaningful, a love of feelings but also intense and noble, a love of power but of a light-giving power, so that there may be love wherever we go!

Love people without committing yourself to their weaknesses.

If you love someone, leave them free! True love extends the human soul.

If you want love to come to you, long for it from your soul's depth. Strong and sincere desires coming from the soul are always fulfilled.

No matter how much you love someone, keep a distance. If you get too close, they will melt you.

*S*tay at a distance so as not to see each other's flaws.
While people are away from each other, they only see their
positive sides. When they get too close they cannot stand each
other.

*E*mbed love into yourselves! Do not talk needlessly! No one
should criticize anyone! Love should be within you! Only
then will you be strong and beautiful! When you learn to
love you will not grow old; you will be young forever.

*L*ove contains the solutions to all
difficult questions. It will come real and
alive, and will sweep away all that is old. One
who knows love is immune to death. Be heroes! Endure
your suffering with ease! Accept and apply love!

*A*pply love in your life in accordance with your own deep
understanding, no matter what people think about it, and do
not impose your understanding upon others.

Be courageous and determined, and talk only of things you have experienced. Do not talk about things that you have not been through. If love fills only your heart, talk of a heart's love; if love fills only your soul, talk of a soul's love; if love fills only your mind, talk of a mind's love; if love fills only your spirit, talk of a spiritual love.

Love should be planted in the soul so that abundance may come. Plant love in your soul and the sources will flow.

Love stays with those who are grateful. Do everything with love. This is why you have come to this world.

Love without expecting to be loved. God blesses every manifestation of love.

Regard each manifestation of love with a sacred thrill, for that is where God is, and where power is.

99

*D*o not talk about your love. Do not tell your beloved that you love them.

*V*alue your friends for the good they do for you. Do not expect from them anything that they cannot give you. Do not tell them how to act, and do not correct them. Leave them free to act as they believe is right.

*I*f you love, do not be distracted. In love, attention should never be diverted.

Enjoy your friends' successes and achievements, but not with a view to taking advantage of them. Do not rearrange things; leave them as God has arranged them.

If you love someone, do not demand that they love only you!

Do not war with love. Love does not seek to make you slaves, but it does not seek to make you saints, either. Those who have love in their hearts and souls have more than a saint's triumph.

*R*egard each other freely and calmly. Some people are
ashamed to love or to speak of their love. Why don't you say,
"I like you a lot?"

*L*ove a person's mind first, then their heart, soul and spirit
and finally their body. If you love a person in this way, they
will love you, too.

*T*hink, feel, but do not talk about love. When your heart becomes as pure as a crystal, your mind as bright as the sun, your soul as noble and vast as the universe, and your spirit as strong as God, only then can you talk of love.

*D*o not keep saying: I love you. Love has a variety of forms in which it can manifest. Bring variety to your love, and your soul will be like a rich garden with many flowers, a great wealth.

Every day, discover new and beautiful features of the mind, the heart and the soul of the person you love. Discover in them new talents, virtues, spiritual wealth, and new values, and your love will constantly grow.

Give up your legalistic morals, and do not judge each other. When you see a man hold or kiss a woman, say "God bless them." If their kiss is an expression of their respect, awe and love, they are doing God's will.

Loving is the soul's work. Do not
meddle in the soul's affairs. Do not be
afraid of love.

Build upon love, put your capital into it, and do not be
afraid. Those who build their lives on love always win. You
cannot meet with danger if you build on love.

If you love someone, do not teach them how to love you, and do not criticize them. If people learned not to interfere with others' love, the world would be a better place.

Do not ask anyone: Do you love me? If you ask, you will lose everything. Who loves you and how is none of your business. It is the other's business. We are concerned with how we love. It is wrong to demand anyone not to love others as well.

Happiness

What takes away your happiness and destroys your noble thoughts, feelings and actions is the absence of love.

If you seek happiness on earth, communicate with people you can rely on in any circumstances, people who would sacrifice themselves for you, who are prepared to go up into the skies and down to earth for you. Do not look for such people; be such a person for others to find.

As long as you live in the world of changes, you cannot expect any happiness.

*S*top in somebody's shadow to rest
and cool down, and you are lost. No one
can make anyone else happy.

*H*appiness is a link between two souls. When two
hearts are properly connected in the right relationship, then as
in music, a tone will form that we call happiness.

*D*o not look for happiness outside yourself. The awakened
seek happiness inside.

*H*appiness is in the person who loves you. If you have a friend who loves you, they will never hurt you.

*T*o be happy, you must love. Love is a condition of achieving happiness. Here on earth we need to build a life of harmony, a society of sober individuals of which it would be a pleasure to be a part. Then, when you meet a person, you will know there is someone that he loves.

*T*he greater your alertness, the greater your opportunity to be happy.

$\mathcal{A}$ttaining happiness is a method, a law deep inside the human soul. How would you arrange your life without happiness? Without happiness, life is a series of disappointments, hardships and suffering. Life has no meaning without happiness.

$\mathcal{B}$eing happy is a great science. If you are not happy, do not be confused. Happiness is hard to achieve.

If you pursue happiness, you are an ordinary person. If happiness pursues you, you are an extraordinary person. Do not chase happiness; let it chase you.

Human happiness is defined by the hardships and conflicts you have been through. The greater they are, the greater is your happiness.

If you have someone who loves you, you are worth more than the richest of kings. If you have someone you can rely upon in any circumstances, that is more than any wealth.

*W*hen I know that someone loves me I feel unhappy. The person who loves me expects something from me, and rightly so. However, if I cannot do what they expect, I suffer. The person who loves me will want to do something for me, and if I cannot do anything for them I am embarrassed and unhappy. When two people love each other and know it, they should do something for each other so that they may be internally free and remove suffering from their path.

Falling in Love

I have a special attitude to falling in love. To me, all people who are in love are treading in a dark night. Their road is bumpy and they keep falling and getting hurt. A person in love never stops falling, and then complains of heartache and ailments. That's what falling in love means.

Do not entangle your heart with others' hearts. Do not fall in love! Love without falling in love.

*F*alling in love is not love. Love
makes you happy and satisfied while
falling in love brings suffering and conflicts.

*P*assing through the body, the supreme vibrations of love
purify it. When you fall in love, a stream of love from the
invisible world passes through you and rejuvenates you.

117

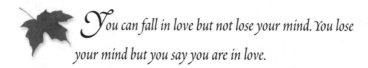 *You* can fall in love but not lose your mind. You lose your mind but you say you are in love.

You fall in love with your neighbor only when he or she is a conduit of something noble and sublime.

Jealousy

*W*hat sort of a love is permeated by jealousy? You are
jealous because you are unaware that everything you need is
inside you.

*B*y not showing your love properly you encounter jealousy
and suffer bitterly.

$\mathcal{P}$eople are afraid of losing what they have. It is from that fear that jealousy originates. What reality can there be where fear is? What sort of a love is it if it can be lost?

$\mathcal{W}$hat does jealousy indicate? Jealousy is love manifested in the physical world. If you are jealous you have a debt to pay; if someone is jealous of you, he has a debt to pay to you.

When does jealousy show up? When love loses the direction God has attributed to it. Through jealousy, you impose on the person you love, and insist that they think of nothing but you. Before demanding from anyone, ask yourself about your own relation with God.

Friendship

If someone is your friend he wants you to grow and
advance in your development, not to make you happy.

*F*riendship brings happiness. Therefore, do everything within
your power to find a friend who loves you and who will stand
firm in any circumstances. This is everyone's task: to be a friend
and to have one.

If you build a friendship with
someone, you should be ready to give them
a part of yourself. Friendship always starts
with giving.

If you wish to befriend someone, look for a person who loves
first God and then themselves. If they love God they will be able
to love their neighbor, too.

125

*O*nly those who are ready to sacrifice themselves for your elevation are your friends.

*G*ive the best of yourself to preserve your friendship.

*F*riendship is a divine feeling, the most sublime experience. A true friend can never do anything that is not for your good.

If you lose the friendship of the person you love, you will lose your light and joy. What will you do without light and joy? A true friend is the one who can help you in the hardest moments of your life. Value your friends by the good they do you.

*O*nly one who has opened their soul and heart for you can be your friend. A true friend is the one who stops your tears and sorrows. When they are around, your suffering and confusion vanish.

127

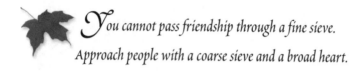

*Y*ou cannot pass friendship through a fine sieve.
Approach people with a coarse sieve and a broad heart.

*W*hen you are unhappy, do not enter your friend's home.

A good friend is worth more than all the wealth in the
world.

Of Flesh,
Passion and Sex

I am not one of those who say that kissing is sinful. A kiss without love, however, is a crime, and every crime entails suffering for the heart or the soul.

A kiss is worthwhile only if it transmits something. A kiss should be a channel of life.

A kiss, depending on its origin, shows how we can be saved from evil in this world.

*I*f someone loves you and directs
their feelings towards you, that is a kiss.

*D*o not kill your flesh or your personality. If you do,
you will remove the conditions for the manifestation of the
divine in your soul. Flesh is the instrument played by the soul.

*W*ithout passion, love can exist but it cannot manifest. In
that case, people suffer. Love does not see the mistakes because it
rectifies them.

*T*he flesh gradually grows stronger. If you follow its laws
you will be wealthy and healthy and will have a good life.

*O*pposing as they may be, the life of the spirit and the life of
the flesh are equally necessary for human development.

The flesh is your old life of which
you cannot rid yourself. If you try to do so,
you will curb your evolution and leave this
world. You cannot ignore your old life, your flesh.

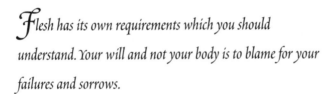

Flesh has its own requirements which you should
understand. Your will and not your body is to blame for your
failures and sorrows.

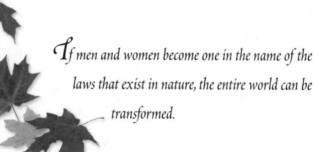

Without the life of the flesh there can be no development. Do not be afraid of the flesh but cultivate it.

Love should first be applied to the physical body just as light and knowledge should be applied to the brain.

If men and women become one in the name of the laws that exist in nature, the entire world can be transformed.

Discover the Magic

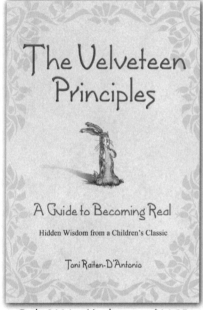

Code 2114 • Hardcover • $14.95

By sharing the timeless insights and poignant quotes from the popular children's book, The Velveteen Rabbit, Toni Raiten-D'Antonio identifies 10 keys to becoming Real, with the promise that when you become Real you will love and be loved with all your strengths, weakness, faults and gifts.

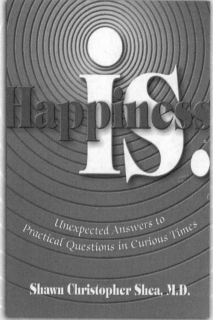